TO:

FROM:

Special thoughts to cheer you up
and cheer you on.

Moments Light and Bright

Fay Angus

illustrated by Peter Church

The C. R. Gibson Company
Norwalk, CT 06856

Laughter is sunshine in the heart
and wings on the soul.

God put twinkles in our eyes, smiles
on our cheeks and gave us the gift
of laughter.

We laugh because people are funny,
life is astonishing, joy is contagious
and God loves us.

And, when we laugh, God laughs with us.

Humor is the tilt of the soul
that keeps us looking up.

A sense of humor is the safety valve
of the human spirit. It...
    breaks up our tensions
    with a well-timed quip...

    deflects our defects with
    a calculated chuckle...

    puts joy into a humdrum task.

Humor is a necessary tonic for the soul.

When we laugh with each other, we work out the kinks in the joints that link us together.

Laughter is an emotional poke in the ribs that blows away our anxieties and tenderizes our tussles.

To lighten up, is to brighten up.

When we can laugh at ourselves, we find
that we are constantly amused.

*Attitudes . . . light and bright and
a little bit breezy, make a heap
o'living a lot more easy!*

When we raise our children on a lap full
of laughter, we program into them the
merry heart that Solomon says is a
"continual feast." It will nourish them
all their lives.

Laughter is God's oil of gladness poured
out over our lives.

Martin Luther kept a flower on his desk. No matter what difficulties he was facing, or internal struggles of his soul, this flower kept him focused on the joy of God's beauty and goodness.

When you were born
the angels sang...
the whole earth smiled
and joybells rang.

Every morning is a Happy Birthday in our lives...the celebration of a brand new beginning.

We can't all be stars...
but we can all twinkle.

Each of us is a unique, one-of-a-kind designer original. We come tagged...

With the compliments of your creator.

God sees us with the eyes of love.

It is a passionate, affirming love that loves us exactly the way we are, but loves us too much to leave us the way we are. It gently moves us from merely *being*, into *becoming* all that we can be.

Written on the fly leaf of my Bible
are the inspiring words of the great
missionary William Carey:

"Expect great things from God!
Attempt great things for God!"

Determination is the staying power that says it's always too soon to give up.

Determination is knowing the limits of your endurance yet taking the hand of faith to stretch beyond them.

Hudson Taylor, founder of the China Inland Mission, focused his determination of purpose into three important words:

"Impossible! Difficult! **DONE**!"

Determination is what separates the winners and losers in life. It is what makes all the difference between swimming and surviving with our nose sometimes only one inch above the water, or sinking and drowning with our nose only one inch beneath the water.

Determination strengthens our survivor instincts. *To survive is to begin again.*

The transitions of our lives are a series of new beginnings. They are a part of the process of becoming. Transitions are the growing of our maturity.

We cannot change the past, but there
is not an experience in life from
which we cannot learn and grow, and which,
when we consecrate to God, He cannot
take and use.

A young man, impressed with the success of a major business figure, approached him . . .

"Sir," he said, "how did you manage to build up this wonderful business?"

"Two words," answered the executive, "right decisions!"

"Ah," replied the young man, "but how did you come to make the right decisions?"

"One word," thundered the executive, "experience!"

"But . . . how did you get the experience?"

"Two words," laughed the executive, "wrong decisions."

Problems are angels
of opportunity in disguise.

A problem is a solution
waiting to rejoice.

When our son Ian was four years old,
he was terrified of the dark. It
seemed that as the sun went down and the
stars came up, a flickering shadow or
rustle of the wind would bring him
ghoulies and ghosties and long-legged
beasties that go bump in the night.

Then at Sunday School, he learned the
"Five Finger Exercise" of Amy Carmichael.

Tap each finger on one hand and
spell out T-R-U-S-T. Then tap
each finger on the other hand
and spell out J-E-S-U-S. Now
clasp your hands together. . .
shut your eyes. . . go to sleep.
You will wake up smiling!

He did.
I did.

I don't know if my son still does
the Five Finger Exercise (he's
a big boy now), but I do.

The Five Finger Exercise is the best
place to start in solving the problems
in our lives. To clasp our hands together
in prayer and trust Jesus to help us.

There is no quick fix for most of the
problems in our lives—God does not
promise us all-at-one successes, but He does
promise us day-to-day encouragement
by His presence and loving care.

Trust is the mainstay of hope.

God seldom does for us that which we can readily do for ourselves, or for other people. He expects us to wrestle down problems in our lives. Problems keep us on the growing edge of faith.

We meet and greet problems every day. As with our own worry lines and frowns, it's hard to keep our spirits up when problems tug them down.

Sometimes problems stare at us
    through other people's eyes,
Those "problem/opportunities,"
    those angels in disguise.

The lonely reaching for a
    kindly word or deed,
The homeless, dispossessed and lost
    that have a special need,
The overburdened and distraught,
The fearful and confused,
The poor, the hungry, the victimized
    who have been badly used.

Lord, take my hands and work
    through them,
Please take my ears to hear.
Take my eyes, my mouth, my heart.
Please show them that we care.

When we are unable to help ourselves
or when no one is able to help us, we
trust God to work His miracles through
our lives.

Bless our hearts, dear Lord, we pray,
with small encouragements day-by-day.
Gentle mercies from above
That wrap us in your arms of love.

Encouragement is the lifeline thrown
from one heart to another to help pull
us through the storms of life.

Encouragement. . .

takes the fragile, quivering and
sometimes broken pieces of our
hearts and holds them in the arms
of prayer.

Encouragement. . .

is a hug and a squeeze when words
are not enough. . .

believes in us and for us when we
are plagued with self-doubt. . .

builds us up and cheers us on.

Encouragement. . .

wades through the murky waters of
our past mistakes and by the quiet
lovelight of its faith teaches us
that God is good, and God is love
and love forgives. . .and forgives.

Encouragement. . .

looks at the very worst in us yet
sees the very best in us, and
when we trip and stumble, it picks
us up, dusts us off and says

Dear Heart—you can begin again!